Destruction to Devotion

ABIGAIL TAYLOR

Copyright © 2022 by Abigail Taylor

All rights reserved.

No part of this book may be reproduced in any form or by any electronic or mechanical means, including information storage and retrieval systems, without written permission from the author, except for the use of brief quotations in a book review.

This is for anyone who has been broken-hearted.

Marks of Sadness

PREFACE

I think we've all experienced a fallout with someone. Whether it's a family member, friend, or lover, it doesn't matter—hurt is hurt. Sometimes people impact us in ways we didn't expect. Maybe they turn our world upside down in the best possible way. Or they turn out to be someone we wish we never met. Either way, their time in our life serves a purpose.

The point is everything happens for a reason, and people affect us long after they're gone. So we need to use our experiences as stepping stones for growth and open our eyes to what the universe is trying to teach us.

I describe my journey across three sections, and this current one covers a painful time in my life that is now far behind me. Hopefully, throughout this part, you will see that even though there are downs, there will also be growth and acceptance.

The message I want to convey is don't lose hope. This is a lesson, not a life sentence, and true, respectful love will find you and light up your world. I assure you the ending is beautiful.

Marks On A Page

I know you won't read this—it's just for me.
This pen and paper have become my therapy.
I write to forget. I'm writing to say sorry.
But it's not about you, so please don't worry.
I'm apologizing to the girl I used to be and for what I put her
through.
For letting her heart get tricked into thinking that she
loved you.
So this is me forgiving myself for the things I can't change.
I'm moving on without you, and I'm turning another page.
With a clean slate, I'm starting a new chapter.
And at the end of this book, I know I'll get my happily ever
after.

Stay With Me

The distance is suffocating me.
Like a weight on my heart, it's making it hard to breathe.
You're here but not near.
I don't understand why you're so far away.
But this is me, on my knees, begging you to stay.

Ride Of Delusion

I feed on the pain you always cause.
It's like you're the drug in my veins, and I get high on your
chaos.
You take me on a roller coaster of emotions, and I can't get
enough of the ups and downs.
I believe all your broken promises, even though they're
nothing more than sounds.
The lows are real low, but I always think just one more fix will
do the trick.
But it's just a delusion, and being with you is my internal
conflict.

Predator

Why do you need to have this power over me? What do you
get out of that?
I'll give you anything you want—all you have to do is ask.
But it's like you live for this cat-and-mouse kind of chase.
Only when I let you catch me, somehow I become the loser in
your twisted game.

Speak To Me

I want to know what you're thinking.
But you say nothing.
The silence tells me something.
But I'm not sure if it's true.
If there's a chance our thoughts are aligned,
Speak now, or I might be gone before you do.

Lost In You

Why do you play these games? Since when are matters of the
heart a competition?
You got that hot-and-cold thing down to an art as if confusing
me was your only mission.
I'm not sure what your prize is or how you keep score.
Do you get points if you think I love you more?
I have to admit, you have my head and heart spinning.
Even when you make me cry, I still want you. Does that mean
you're winning?
I'm not someone who normally cares if I lose as long as I get to
play.
But I so desperately wanted to win your love that I lost myself
along the way.

Changing Space

Sometimes I just want to cry to see if you even care.
Will you ask me what's wrong or pretend like I'm not there?
You don't touch me like you used to.
Is that a sign we're through?
What will it take for you to notice me?
Do I need to be someone else entirely?
I don't understand how we ended up this way.
You're so distant and cold. Do you even want to stay?
When did our home turn into such a sterile place?
It's like we're just coexisting in the same space.
Are we really over, or are we going to give it another try?
I guess I got my answer when you walked away and watched
me cry.

Who Are You?

Your smile could wash away all my tears, but you keep it
hidden behind your disguise.
You stand there watching me with nothing but a vacant gaze
in your eyes.
Looking so cold, you've become a person I don't even
recognize.
I need to know what happened to us, but all I hear are lies.
We stare right through each other as if we're saying our silent
goodbyes.

Addicted

You're this habit I feed deep inside of me.
Taking over and consuming who I used to be.
I don't fight it because I know it's no use.
You take what you want, and I enjoy the abuse.
The torture is love, and it swallows me whole.
I feel you inside and out and everywhere I go.
Greedily, you feast as I turn the other cheek.
My guard is down, as you have made me weak.

Deafened By Doubts

Whoever said silence was golden didn't know you.
Because when you don't talk, it makes me question everything
I did or didn't do.
I want to hear the words inside your head,
But I'm met with a voiceless sound instead.
Your quiet response is loud enough to break my heart.
Who knew words unsaid could tear my world apart?

Honesty

Please don't sugarcoat how you feel.
Let your guard down and just be real.
Talk to me and tell me what to do?
I've never been more scared of losing you.
I literally feel you slipping away.
But if I'm not what you want, how can I beg you to stay?

Guilty Silence

You lied because you thought it would hurt me less.
But that wasn't what I wanted. I needed you to confess.
Hearing the words is the only thing that will set me free.
How else will I know if it's the end of you and me?
I know you're worried that what you'll say will tear us apart.
But not knowing the truth is literally breaking my heart.

Defeated

I don't think I can do this anymore.
I thought I knew what I wanted, but now I'm not so sure.
You said things to me that tore my world in two.
Now, the only thing I know is I need time away from you.
I never thought I'd be that girl who had to make this kind of
choice.
Your actions were like a gut punch to the stomach, causing me
to lose my voice.
I'm left crying in my room, feeling angry and confused and
defeated.
There must have been a misunderstanding when I heard you
say, "I'm sorry, I cheated."

Left Behind

Just when I think I'm fine, waves of sadness crash over me. Did
I mean anything to you at all?
You dismissed me without a second thought. But first, you
made me feel special—you made me fall.
I was a fool who saw what I wanted to see.
That there was no one else, even though I knew it wasn't true.
Just when I think I'm fine, waves of sadness crash over me.
I'll never be fine again, and that's all because of you.

What's Wrong With Me?

You tell me to breathe, but then you steal the air from me.
I'm not sure how I ended up in this place again, yet here I am.
Anyone I ever get close to chooses to leave—what's wrong
with me?
The pain I feel is very real, even if it's just in my mind.
It is that emotional heartbreak turned physical kind.

Ghosted

You promised forever, but I had no idea forever would end.
One day you were here. The next day you were gone like the
wind.
You escaped like a thief in the night, stealing a piece of me
along the way.
Now, I'm just a ghost of who I was, wondering how I could've
made you stay.

Hooked On You

You're like a drug that I physically crave.
I let what you claimed was love course through my veins.
Once I was hooked on that euphoric high, you took it all away.
You left without warning while I writhed in pain.
Just when I detoxed, you seeped back into my system.
I'm weak, and I can't quit you even if I try—I'm forever your
victim.

Broken

They say pain is temporary, but not when it comes to the
heart.
That kind of hurt doesn't know how to stop once it starts.
My world turned upside down the day you left and would
never be right again.
I took for granted all the time we had together, and now it has
come to an end.
Moving on is impossible for me to do, because I'm broken
beyond repair after losing you.
My pieces will never fit back together as you've left me in this
world alone forever.

Lost In Sadness

Sadness comes in waves that you just can't understand.
You put on a happy face, but that doesn't change the way you feel.
Push it down, don't let it out. Maybe things will work out as planned.
Years ago, you pictured your perfect life: happiness, joy, love.
But today, the people and things that surround you seem like props.
As if you're looking through someone else's eyes, watching from above.
You shouldn't feel this way; you're so lucky, that's what they all say.
The smiles never reach your eyes, and sorrow is buried deep within.
So push it down, don't let it out. Maybe it will all go away.
You don't know the pressure that surrounds me.
My life might seem like it's all together,
But I'm carrying a weight you can't see.
You want to do something, anything, just to know you're alive.
Life moves but, in your mind, you're standing still.

Try to push it down, don't let it out, and maybe you'll survive.
Waking up each day, you hope that the hurt won't continue to be inside.
But it's hard to focus, to listen, to even remember to breathe.
And as soon as you're alone, the tears want to flow like a landslide.
You know if just one escapes, more will come, and it will never end.
You slowly inhale, count to ten, and tell yourself the pain isn't real.
If you push it down, don't let it out, then maybe this can all be pretend.
Look around you; find out who you are and who you want to be.
Things can and will be better, if only you believe.
Open your eyes to the things you have and really try to see.
Feelings don't have to own you, and things can go your way.
Cry if you need to, smile for real, love deeply, and laugh loudly.
Just don't push it down, let it out, and everything will be okay.

Disturbed

Sleep is like a mistress that slips away in the night, as my
anxious mind won't give me any peace.
Thoughts of you pound in my brain of their own accord like
they're begging for release.
My breathing comes hard like a jackhammer beating on my
chest.
Thump, thump, thump. It's my worries knocking, causing
this unrest.
I feel powerless to these emotions that refuse to take a break.
I try to turn a blind eye, but there's no hope as I continue to
stay awake.

Without Love

Love isn't blind, it's dangerous.
You can't see what's right in front of you—you're oblivious.
It numbs you to pain by offering you passion.
But when it's gone, you're left with a hurt you couldn't
imagine.
There's no medicine to take, and there's really nothing you
can do.
But just like any drug, if you're not careful, love will be the
death of you.

Second Place

The things you said that made me feel special were nothing
but lies.
All so you could win a game I didn't even know we were
playing.
Now I'm left sitting on the sidelines.
Holding my broken heart as a consolation prize.

Abandoned

You once asked me what my biggest fear was.
I told you that people would leave me.
You said, "I'm not going anywhere," as you walked away.

Painful Silence

I know misery is supposed to love company,
But I need to know you are doing better than me.
Because I wouldn't wish this feeling on my worst enemy.

Blindsided

You hurt me—that's a fact; you played me for a fool.
I was blindsided by your betrayal because I never thought a
person could be so cruel.
You said you loved me, but that was just an act; you only ever
loved you.
Now that you're out of my life, I can see how nothing about
our relationship was true.

Shattered

I tried to give you what I thought you wanted.
But you still left, and now I'm feeling haunted.
The ghost of our relationship dances inside my brain.
But if I'm being honest, I kinda like the pain.
The hurt lets me know I still have a beating heart.
Even if it's shattered to pieces and all but falling apart.

Still Healing

Remember when you moved on and thought that person was
out of your life forever?
Then you hear a song that rips your heart out of your chest,
reminding you of your time together.

Empty

I no longer know who I am.
When I was with you, I felt whole.
But now I just feel the hole you left in me that can't be filled—
not even with tears.
And I know because I've already tried.

Cornered

We drown ourselves in fake promises that are really the devil in
disguise.
Sometimes we need to feel the pain of rock bottom before we
ever realize.
Without the hurt to show we're still alive even if we're not
doing well.
We might give up altogether and follow our demons straight
into hell.
Our bodies can put up with a lot, but it's our minds that are
open to the greatest attack.
So even though the bad looks good, our suffering lets us know
we have to fight back.

Alone

I don't know where to go while I wander down this lonely
road.
I'm trying to find my way, but everything is closed.
It's been over a year now. Is anyone else out there, or is a life of
solitude my true destiny?
If I squint into the distance, is that hope or just an illusion—
my mind playing tricks on me?
The time ticks by so slowly that I wonder if this is all a horrible
dream.
But then I wake up, and nothing changes—me, home alone,
and I want to scream.
There's no one to share in my worries, no one to understand
my pain.
I'll keep searching for comfort, but it seems to me that
everything remains the same.

Is This The End?

I'm low, way down low, below the ground I go.
I thought I could drink the memories away, but in my head is
where they stay.
I long for the day when I'm indifferent, but nothing seems to
make me forget.
I need emotional novocaine to try to numb this internal pain.
The hurt seems to cut through me, and I don't know where to
start.
But now I'm walking around like the Tin Man, just searching
for my heart.

Silently Sinking

I can't take all of this uncertainty surrounding me.
I feel like I'm losing control.
My mind is screaming for help, but it's the words I withhold.
There is no one in sight to hear my silent cries.
As fear floods my body and drowns me inside.
I'm all alone, trying to fight, but everything seems so heavy.
All these emotions are coming at once, and I'm afraid they'll
break the levee.
I don't know if they'll suck me under or wash me to shore.
But I do know something has got to give because I can't take it
anymore.

Fighting Back

I'm falling apart, ripping at the seams.
Internally I'm struggling—there's a sharp pain inside, but that
lets me know my will is strong.
Keep going—I can't give in to that little voice telling me I need
to stop what I'm doing and move on.
The hunger tugs deep inside, demanding to be heard.
But I ignore it and feel powerful, only physically I'm weak and
crumbling, needing the one thing I'm fighting against.
This battle is real, but no matter what I do, even if I feel like
I'm winning, I lose.

Stained Forever

My eyes are open, but I'm still dreaming you're here.
I lick my lips, and I taste your bitterness in the air.
The smell of your betrayal still lingers in my nose.
The sound of your lies rings out as if you were close.
I repeatedly blink to send you on your way, but you refuse to leave.
Closing my eyes tight, I take a deep breath and count to three.
When I open them again, I no longer see you, but not because you aren't there.
Instead, there's a waterfall cascading down my face that hides your vacant stare.
I'm wishing that I never met you and I could erase our time together.
But I know you'll never be gone because you've stained my heart forever.

The Final Act

The lies dripped from your mouth like the blood from the
knife you stabbed in my back.
When you said you'd protect my heart, I had no idea you
meant ripping it from my chest and taking it with you as you
walked out the door.
I guess leaving me bleeding out was what you meant when you
said till death do us part.

Lost In Silence

All of our unsaid thoughts hang in the air like a thick fog,
clouding our vision of what could be.
Lurking in the mist are the shadows of unresolved feelings that
will eventually leave us in a haze of regret.
But if we clear the air, will we find each other, or will it just
open our eyes to what's truly there—nothing?

Where Did You Go?

I was on my knees, begging for you to stay.
Broken couldn't begin to describe me when you just walked
away.
I crawled under the covers and wished I'd never met you.
With no one around, I only had the voices in my head to
talk to.
Praying this was all a nightmare and I'd wake up with you next
to me.
I rolled over, but nothing was there, just a ghost of what used
to be.

Choked by Sadness

Your words were like a noose around my heart.
Choking the life out of my happy ending.
How can we be over before we even start?
When you said I love you, were you just pretending?
I don't understand how you went from falling to leaving so
fast.
You have me questioning everything you ever said.
Did you know from the beginning we wouldn't last?
It's like you got what you wanted and then fled.

Thrill Of The Hunt

You wanted all of my attention until I gave it to you.
Then you pushed me away and told me not to.
I got your message loud and clear—you want me to leave you
alone.
Don't worry, I won't come around, and I've already deleted
your pictures from my phone.
It's funny how things can be so good and then make a
complete one-eighty.
But maybe they were never what they seemed, and I was just
crazy.
Crazy to believe that you actually wanted me.
But I was just the thrill of the hunt, and now I'm a casualty.

Losing Game

My brain's a mess, and my heart's worse.
It's like loving you has been my greatest curse.
Why can't things between us ever be calm?
But it's like when you put us together, we're a firebomb.
Ready to explode the first chance we get.
Ending in feelings of sadness and regret.
You're mad, I yell—we both end up in tears.
But not being together is still my greatest fear.

Emotional Scars

I have a lot on my mind, and I know how I am.
When I'm down, my thoughts will get out of hand.
Spiraling toward a hole of despair.
Not much can stop me now—I'm already there.
The tears well up, but nothing falls, and I'm not sure why.
The feeling is agonizing, but it's like I'm too sad to even cry.
Crawling into bed as if I could sleep away the pain.
I want to forget everything and shut off my brain.
Why do these waves of emotions have to hit me so hard?
I guess it's just something you deal with when you're
internally scarred.

My Struggle

It's weird how something unseen can have so much weight.
Like a force pushing the air from your lungs, causing you to
suffocate.
Taking a deep breath is the hardest thing for you.
Yet it's what everyone is telling you to do.
It would be nice to be able to relax and let it all go.
But unfortunately, the anxiety you caused has a mind of
its own.

Estranged

Remember when we used to talk every day?
Now, if I bumped into you, I wouldn't even know what
to say.
We are just strangers who used to love each other in another
life.
I don't recognize the person you are or that vacant stare in
your eyes.
I can't believe we made a U-turn right into a dead end.
But now you're gone, and I didn't just lose a lover, I lost my
best friend.

New Beginnings

How could the universe get it so wrong?
I thought you were the one, but I haven't heard from you in so
long.
Time erased all the good memories but left all the pain.
Giving me a reminder that I never want you around me again.
Your leaving turned out to be a blessing in disguise.
However, it took me falling to rock bottom to realize.
You probably think about the day you left without saying
goodbye.
But all I think about is the first day I woke up and didn't cry.
That was the beginning of my new life with you as a distant
memory.
I'm not even sorry I met you because I learned a valuable
lesson from your disloyalty.

Wounded Words

I can't believe how many words I've bled.
Hoping it would get her out of my head.
I poured my soul onto this paper.
Doing anything I could just to escape her.
But nothing I did would let me forget.
Now I'm stuck with a life of regret.

Exposed

You knew me better than anyone.
I gave you my heart, and you broke it just for fun.
But the lies you told weren't just to me.
They were to her, to yourself, to everybody.
I hope you sleep well, knowing we all see the truth.
But you can keep your sorries to yourself, for your actions
have no excuse.

Haunted By Heartbreak

Heartbreak comes and floods my mind, body, and spirit.
I knew I should have kept my heart closed and never let you
near it.
Now I'm just a ghost of who I was, and I can never go back.
No matter what I do, I am changed, and I will forever bleed
black.

Destruction

Your lies were weapons of mass destruction—hurting even the
people who had your back.
And I'm left sifting through the wreckage after this tragic
attack.
You didn't care what happened, as long as you got what you
craved.
Now, I'm looking around for survivors, but all I see are graves.

You're To Blame

Your disloyalty was like a knife in my back that went straight
to my heart.
You never said a word while you watched everything around
me fall apart.
As I crumbled to the ground, I tried to figure out what had
happened.
But it was too late. My world went dark—everything had
blackened.
I never saw it coming, as it was a cowardly attack.
There was nothing I could do, no time to react.
At least I went in peace, knowing I wasn't the one to blame.
I hope you feel guilty because you can't say the same.

Two Souls Betrayed

Does she know you told me we were soul mates and made for
each other?
That us meeting was the universe saying that we belonged
together.
I know it's wrong, and I should remove myself from the
situation.
But I'm in too deep, and I can't handle the separation.
My head says leave, but my heart doesn't want to.
Deep down, I know we both deserve better than you.
My world's fucked up, and I can't let you go.
Even though you'll never be mine to have and to hold.
No matter how you look at it, I'm the bad guy.
Even if I'm just a pawn in your game of lies.

Time Heals

I go back and forth. Some days are better than others.
Most of the time I don't even miss you, but other times I
suffer.
Your memory will always be with me, but it will fade over
time.
And the day will come when I won't even remember when
you used to be mine.

Forever Guilty

My mind's destructive, and these thoughts border on
obsessive.
Where do I begin? Why did I let you in?
How could you be so cold? What other lies have you told?
Who did you love all along? When did this all go wrong?
These questions circle around my brain, but they're making
me insane.
I can't focus on anything but you and all that you put me
through.
Did you ever feel the same, or was this all just part of your
game?
You found my insecurity and then used it against me.
I'll never understand the point of your deceitful plans.
But it doesn't matter because my blood will forever stain your
hands.

Forgiveness

I cried a thousand tears, and each one was for you.
A thousand questions passed, wondering what I should do.
Hurt turned into hatred, and that animosity lived inside
of me.
I cried a thousand tears, knowing I wasn't the person I wanted
to be.
You weren't worth my thoughts yet I couldn't let you go.
You were long gone, but somehow still in control.
Forgiveness was my saving grace that finally set me free.
And that was the one thing I gave you that was only for me.

Healing Grace

PREFACE

Grieving is a never-ending road, and there are times when you think you've moved on, but something as simple as a song can bring back those feelings of anguish. But the thing that I have found is that even though the journey is bumpy and there are setbacks, as time goes on, the snags seem to be fewer and farther between. And when they do happen, they don't hit nearly as hard.

What's important to realize is it doesn't matter how long it takes to feel better as long as you continue moving on. The shell of a person you once were will become whole again. Maybe you'll meet some friends who help pull you out of the darkness. Or maybe you do some self-reflection and self-care and find that you never needed anyone because you had everything inside of you all along. Regardless of how you progress, the point is, you do.

In this next selection of poems, I wrote about not only someone who helped me see things from a different perspective but how I wanted to be seen. I hope my words convey the ups and downs of the healing process, but also show that there are more highs than lows.

Smile Through The Pain

Smile—today is a new day.
Smile—because you're worth so much more than the pain.
Smile—happiness is a state of mind and you can decide.
Smile—you're stronger than you know.
So wear your smile like a suit of armor and show it off
everywhere you go.

Gift To Yourself

Love comes so easily when it's for someone else.
But before you freely give your love away.
Remember that no one can love you as good as you can love
yourself.

Tormented Soul

I know we live two different lives,
But it's like I still feel you every time I close my eyes.
Even though you're gone, I still wish you were with me.
Maybe if I close my eyes tighter, you really could be.
I know it will never happen, and I need to accept that.
You left me, and I realize you're never coming back.
I should be over you, but the truth is, I'm not.
Maybe one day, you won't be the one that I want.
But for now, no one needs to know what happens when I
dream.
As long as I keep smiling, maybe one day I'll be as happy as I
seem.

Moving On

I wasn't sure it would happen, but here I am... over you.
Now I'm doing the one thing I didn't think I could do.
I'm closing the door on who I used to be.
That girl is gone, and this woman now is the real me.
I learned a lot when I had to pick myself up off the floor.
And I realized that I don't need you anymore.
Our meeting was like a whirlwind, and your leaving was just as fast.
And like a tornado, you destroyed everything in your path.
But I survived that natural disaster, and I'm stronger than ever.
So thank you for leaving because now my life is better.

Edging Forward

This is not goodbye. You won't get anything good from me
ever again.
I'm sneaking away in the night as an act of silent revenge.
I'm no longer agonizing or angry or anything toward you.
As I walk away, I realize you're not even in my rearview.
I've gone so far down this road that I'm finally free.
And no longer on the path of self-loathing. Instead, I've
moved on to self-discovery.

Healing

I was shards of sharp jagged edges, designed to keep people
at a distance.
But you ignored my brokenness and rescued me, pushing
through
my resistance.
You filled my cracks with understanding, kindness,
and affection.
Fixing what I thought was damaged beyond repair—taking my
life in a
new direction.
I've been confused before, but that feels like love to me.

A Beautiful Scar

They say that damaged attracts damaged, and maybe they're
right.
But I promise I'll be by your side and never let you go without
a fight.
So what if you're broken—I am too, but when our souls
collide, we'll make it through.
We don't need someone else to complete who we are.
We've put ourselves back together, and all that remains from
the pain is a beautiful scar.

Patience, Please

I know my heart's scarred and has been beaten and bruised.
It'll never be perfect and needs constant repairs because it's
been abused.
But if you're patient with me while I try to fix what was
broken, I promise to make it shiny and new.
It might not seem like much, a used heart, but it's all I have,
and I'm giving it to you.

Our Secret Place

I wish I could erase all the memories that haunt you.
Pretend the past never existed before us two.
We can go to that place where we first met.
The one without any doubt or regret.
Where we let our guards down and each other in.
You remember? Where we first became friends.
We laughed until we cried and never felt broken.
We had this connection and let our hearts be open.
Moving away from all the people who caused us pain.
This is the place I wish we could always remain.

Devoted

I understand you're still hurting, and that's okay.
Trying to forget the past doesn't make it go away.
But you can always talk to me, and I'll do my best to
understand.
And even if I don't, I'll still be there, listening and holding
your hand.
I want you to trust me, but I know it's something I have to
earn.
I'll always be there for you and never expect anything in
return.
I know you're scared to give up control because you wear it
like a shield.
But I promise you're safe with me, and I'll guard your heart
even after it has healed.

Happiness

Let today be the day you forgive and release the anger you're
holding on to.
Relieve yourself of all that pain because that's what happy
people do.

I Found Me

A year has passed, and if I'm honest, it seems like a lifetime.
When I wake up each morning, you don't even cross my mind.
I thought you broke my heart, and I hated you for leaving.
But now I realize those feelings were all a part of grieving.
I'm stronger now and happier than I thought I could be.
And I'm glad that I lost you because I finally found me.

Thank You

You helped me when I was at my worst.
I wish it was you who I'd met first.
She took so much from me, but you gave me more.
Putting me back together, piece by piece, you picked me up off
the floor.
The damage was done, but you never saw me as broken.
My heart was closed, but your tenderness gently pried it open.
Being with you breathed life into me when there was literally
none.
And you turned this ghost of a person back into a human.

You're Mine

I had scars so deep I didn't think they would ever heal.
But you came out of nowhere and changed the way I feel.
You taught me to embrace my pain and turn it into art.
You were a bandage for my soul and fixed my broken heart.
I still remember the day I woke up, and she wasn't my first thought.
Instead, it was you on my mind because you're the only one I want.

A Beautiful Wreck

Every day I woke up, it was hard to get out of bed.
The pain crushed my chest as your betrayal danced through
my head.
You left without warning or even giving a reason why.
Everything reminded me of you, and I felt like I could die.
Shattered into a million pieces was all that I could see.
But she showed me I was whole and who I was supposed to be.
I quickly forgot all about you and how you did me wrong.
She made me realize that without you, I was actually strong.
I was no longer this broken emotional wreck.
She helped me understand I didn't need to live life with regret.
Obviously, I was supposed to meet you and have you break my
heart.
Because if I didn't, I wouldn't have been able to appreciate her
from the start.

Free From Deceit

The pain was excruciating and made me feel like I was dying.
Maybe I was on the inside, but on the outside, I just kept
crying.
But one day, everything changed, and it couldn't be explained.
Someone came and rescued me from my internal prison.
They washed away the hurt as they sat there and listened.
Never judging me for what I did or didn't do.
They just made me see that I was better off without you.
Showing me what they saw through unbiased eyes.
I was able to move on and escape your web of lies.

Saved From Drowning

You came into my life when I was weak and needed direction.
Breaking down my walls, you lowered my inhibition.
I trusted you and fell harder than I thought possible.
You made me believe you loved me and together we were
unstoppable.
I thought you had rescued me, but really you just let me
drown.
You left without even caring that you turned my world upside
down.
Then someone threw a life preserver and helped me out of the
deep end.
With no regard for herself, she saved me even though she
couldn't swim.
Just when I thought it was all over and I couldn't see the light.
She pulled me to safety and wouldn't let me give up the fight.
I'm thankful for her because she stood by me during my
darkest days.
You may have broken me, but she was the glue that held
together my remains.

The Power Of Love

Love can heal, but it can also destroy.
It can bring unending pain as well as insurmountable joy.
It's a powerful weapon that can bring the strongest person to
their knees.
Love is a drug that can consume someone like a disease.
I've seen love cause tears of ecstasy as well as agony.
Can you think of a greater dichotomy?

Let Freedom Ring

I go through life, and nothing's as it seems.
I only know how to exist at extremes.
When I'm down, it's the lowest you can be.
But when I'm up, I'm like a bird flying free.
I want to feel safe and settled in reality.
I'm tired of constantly searching for things I can't see.
Starting today, I'm living life my way.
I'm getting off this roller coaster ride, and I'm no longer going to hide.
I've been pretending for far too long that I'm okay.
But I'm officially over you, and this is my independence day.

Open The Door

Let me inside the dark recesses of your brain.
I want to find the source of your pain.
I'll do everything I can to make it better.
I'll help you forget that you ever met her.
With me, there's nothing you need to hide.
So loosen your tongue and don't keep it tied.

Lost In You

You always broke your promises to me.
Yet, I believed every word you would say.
When I was with you, I forgot who I was supposed to be.
You loved control and always had to have things your way.
We'd fight, then break up, which is what we should've done.
But then you'd come around apologizing, begging me to take
you back.
I'd listen to the lies you spewed and would get caught in the
web you spun,
But it never failed. You'd say all the right things, and
eventually, I'd crack.
This back-and-forth wasn't really love, but it was all I ever
knew.
Until I met someone who showed me what I truly deserved,
which was someone better than you.

Fighting Back

My mind is a train, going nowhere fast.
I wonder how long these feelings of uncertainty will last.
I hear random thoughts dance inside my head.
Speaking words to me that no one ever said:
You're not good enough, and no one will ever love you.
But when I look at my life, I know the words aren't true.
They are just lies that live inside of me and constantly get me
off track.
But I won't let them win. I'm stronger than I used to be, and
this time I'm fighting back.

My Everything

You're my safe place when my dangerous mind threatens to
trap me.
You make my world better than I ever thought it could be.
You pulled me from the undertow and brought me to shore.
You've seen me at my very worse but loved me even more.
You're my peace when there's nothing but chaos around.
You are the only person who can lift me up when I'm down.
You've given me something better than my wildest dream.
You took the two pieces of my heart and repaired the broken
seam.

Your Love

Your eyes drink me in and take away my insecurity.
I tell you, "I'm not perfect," and you say, "You are to me."
How you can see more than this person who is broken and
flawed, I'll never understand.
I didn't imagine opening myself up to you, but not everything
goes as planned.
I worry that you'll wake up one day and realize I'm not the
person you believe.
But when that day comes, I'm going to hold on tight and beg
you not to leave.
I've always been closed off, and I never meant to feel this way.
But you break more of my walls down every time you choose
to stay.

Here For You

You continuously fight the battles for others even though
you're facing your own war.
You inspire so many, but you don't have to pretend to be
strong anymore.
I can be your rock, and I'll never leave your side.
I know you're hurting, but with me, you don't have to hide.
You can lay your worries on me, and my love will still remain.
I want to be your sweet escape—the antidote to your pain.

Fix Me

Holding together all of my broken pieces is exhausting.
Living this fake existence is more than daunting.
But you found me and took away my pain.
And now, my life will never be the same.
You unshackled me from these chains and showed me a world
I never knew.
I no longer have to hold myself together because that's what
you do.

Confession

I want you to know all of my issues before going into this.
I don't want your judgment to be clouded by ignorant bliss.
You need to be prepared because I'm a hard pill to swallow.
I may seem like I'm whole, but inside I'm hollow.
I keep my feelings bottled up because I hate confrontation.
If I get scared, I'll leave without any hesitation.
I have a bad temper, and my emotions can get out of hand.
This is just the tip of the iceberg, but I need you to
understand.
I'm trying to be honest and lay it all out for you to see.
Being with me isn't easy, but I hope you'll look past my flaws
and still want me.

All Mine

I never understood jealousy.
It's one emotion that's lost on me.
If you're jealous, does that mean you care?
Because to me, it means that trust isn't there.
But if you're not jealous, are you lacking passion?
To show love, does it have to be in an all-consuming fashion?
I never understood jealousy... but now I think I do.
Because it makes me physically ill to think of anyone else
with you.

Exposed

I wish I hadn't shown you all the sides of me.
Especially the one with my vulnerability.
But with you, my resolve is weak
And my mind doesn't think before I speak.
My openness is both a blessing and a curse.
But it makes me feel like I'm loving in reverse.
I give myself to you but pull away when you get too close.
I tell you my secrets that no one else knows.
Will seeing the real me make you want to leave?
Why did I have to go around wearing my heart on my sleeve?

Hurtful Truths

You say I'm obsessive, and I know that's true.
Might as well add passive-aggressive and needy, too.
I'm hard to be with, I won't try to deny.
But you told me you'd still love me. Was that just a lie?
Sometimes you say things you think I want to hear.
But I only want the truth, just so we're clear.
Your words might hurt, and that's okay.
I'd rather you be honest and leave than lie and stay.

An Empty Space

I was done thinking of you, so how did you manage to creep
into my brain?
Now all the memories come rushing back, flooding me with
emotions I can't explain.
I'm so over being a victim of how I feel.
But I don't know how to numb the pain so I can heal.
The path I'm on isn't linear—it's zigzagged.
This never-ending journey has me feeling jet-lagged.
I'm ready to get off this ride and just move on.
But I can't seem to fill the void you created now that you're
gone.

Will You Stay?

You can't fix me, so please don't try.
My issues stack up miles high.
I could start a list, but I know what that would do.
Scare you away just like everyone before you.
I wish I could find someone who embraced my flaws and really
understood.
Someone who wouldn't bail the first time that things were less
than good.
There's a reason I only show one dimension instead of three.
I'm better in print than in person, and you'd be disappointed
in the real me.

Stay With Me

I'm sorry I let you down.
I have issues from before you were around.
I want you to know I'm doing my best to move on.
But sometimes my past dictates how I respond.
I don't want that to mess up what we've created.
And I understand why you get so frustrated.
I realize you are nothing like her and never could be.
I love you, and I'm begging that you don't give up on me.

Insomniac

It's 2:00 a.m., and I'm wide awake, thinking of you.
Are you doing the same and thinking of me, too?
I must be lonely, but how could I be?
I'm surrounded by people, but they don't know me.
I beg my brain to shut off, to stop all these questions that I
can't answer.
But it just speeds up and continues hopping around like a tiny
tap dancer.
I pray that sleep comes to me. Instead, I see your face.
But you already know that, as you've found every hidden
place.
I turn toward the clock—it's 3:00 a.m., and I need to get some
rest.
But there are so many things I need to get off of my chest.
Even though there's nothing in my mind that would come as a
surprise.
Because you are always there, every time I close my eyes.

Still Healing

I know our story isn't the same.
But those unwanted thoughts creep into my mind, and she's
to blame.
She took me down a long and dark road, leaving me
emotionally dead.
Now you have to suffer with all the insecurities floating inside
my head.
I realize it isn't fair that you get the damaged version of me.
But she got to me first and took the best of who I used to be.
I want to change, and if I could for anyone, it would be you.
So please don't give up on me—I just have a little healing left
to do.

Thoughts

Your love is pulling me under, making it hard to breathe.
I worry you'll wake up and realize you're too good for me.
What happens when you remove the rose-colored glasses and
finally see?
See that I'm not the person you want me to be.
And that I'm really just broken and flawed to the nth degree.
These are the thoughts that float through my mind every time
you leave.

Our Road Trip

What can I do to put your mind at ease?
I know it feels like you've been here before, but I'm a one-way
street.
There's no turning around—I want us to always progress.
You're at the wheel, and you know the address.
The only rule is the longer you travel, the faster you go.
I need you with me, so please don't take it slow.
I know you're scared, but the only person on this road is you.
And I promise to keep you safe, no matter what I have to do.
If you continue, your final destination will be my heart.
But if that's not your ultimate goal, then please don't even
start.

My Safe Place

The clock ticks by, and my heart races.
So many bodies—so many empty faces.
Looking for an escape just to get some air.
Surrounded by people, but none of them care.
It's overstimulation at its best, and I need to be alone so I can
get some rest.
Taking me away and wrapping me in your body.
You save me from the anxiety of this party.
My nerves calm as I melt into you.
There's no one else around—it's just us two.
This is my safe place right here in your arms.
You're the only one who can shelter me from my internal
storms.

My Savior

Remember when you thought you'd be happier without me?
Leaving me blindsided by your disloyalty.
You ripped my heart out as you turned and walked away.
Never even checking my pulse to see if I was okay.
But then, an angel brought me back to life.
Healing my wounds and removing your knife.
Breathing happiness and love into everything I do.
Making me see that I'm better off without you.
So, in the end, your selfishness worked out in my favor.
Because it gave me a chance to find my true savior.

Please Wait

My heart wasn't broken—it was shattered.
I didn't know if it would ever be whole again.
But then I met you, and I felt like I mattered.
Even though I'm struggling to let you in.
I hope you won't give up on me just yet.
I want you to know I'm doing the best I can do.
I realize I'm a wild card and not a safe bet.
But I promise I'm trying to be better for you.

Safe In Your Arms

You tell me to bend, but I'm afraid I will break.
You want me to give, but what will they take?
You tell me to pretend, but I can't be fake.
You want me to live, but what if it's a mistake?
I had no idea life could be so hard, and I would have to walk
around beaten and scarred.
You tell me, "It's okay to feel this way. Everybody does from
time to time.
But know that you're safe with me, and I'll always protect
what is mine."

Here With You

I know you can fight this fight on your own.
But let me be the one to pull the sword from the stone.
I know you're strong; you don't have to prove it to me.
But if you give me your burdens, I can make your pain less
heavy.
I know you think everyone went AWOL.
But you're wrong. I'll be by your side through it all.

Healed Hearts

Our hearts are fragile, that's why they're kept in cages.
But when it gets broken, it seems like nothing ever changes.
Until someone comes along and picks up the pieces,
Putting you back together and leaving you speechless.
The gentle way they cradle your heart in their hand.
You know they'd never cause you pain because they truly
understand.
No one can love you better than someone who's been hurt
before.
Now that we've found each other, we don't have to be part of
the broken hearts club anymore.

Don't be Scared

I wish you'd tell me exactly how you feel.
The emotions are there, but it's the words you won't reveal.
You have these silent worries that you don't talk about.
But if I don't know, how will I be able to ease your doubt?
I hope to assuage your fear just by always being here.
But it's like you're building up walls to keep me away.
As if you're testing me to see if I'll break them down and stay.
You're used to a self-fulfilling prophecy, but that was before
you met me.
When I say I'm going to do something, I do.
And I meant it when I said I'll never hurt you.

Looking Back

When you left, I wasn't sure I could go on.
One minute you were here, the next you were gone.
My life turned upside down when you walked out.
Leaving me hopeless and filled with doubt.
I never thought I would feel the same way again.
Which is good because I'm happier than I've ever been.
You took a part of me with you when you closed that door.
But you can have it because I never want to be her anymore.

My Liberation

Before I met you, I felt like I was drowning.
Lost at sea with nothing to protect me.
Then you came like a hurricane, washing me to land.
Never had the air been so free than when you held me in your
hands.
Being with you was my salvation—your love, my liberation.
So I'm begging you to hold on tight and never let me go.
If you don't, I'm afraid I'll get caught in the undertow.

Full Circle

They say people come into your life for a reason.
Maybe to show you how to love or teach you a lesson about
leaving.
I no longer question why someone didn't choose to stay.
I know what I have to offer, and I've found that person who'll
never stray.
I'm glad these people were temporary, even if they left
permanent marks.
Because now that they're gone, I'm able to give her my whole
heart.

Finding Happiness

When you left, I wasn't sure I could go on.
One minute you were here, the next you were gone.
My life turned upside down when you walked out.
Leaving me hopeless and filled with doubt.
I never thought I would feel the same way again,
Which is good because I'm happier than I've ever been.
You took a piece of me with you when you closed that door.
But you can have it because I never want to be that person
anymore.

Hard To Love

I'm hard to love.
At least that was what you led me to believe.
I'm hard to love.
Why else would you up and leave?
I'm hard to love.
Even though I gave you every part of me.
I'm hard to love.
Although I didn't think I should be.
I'm hard to love.
That was what your actions used to say.
But is that true?
No, it was your insecurity reflecting back at me that made me
feel that way.

Goodbye

Staring over the edge, my thoughts are dancing like the world
below.
It's a reminder that everything in life will eventually come
and go.
We're not guaranteed tomorrow, so we have to live for today.
Is that what you were thinking when you turned and walked
away?
I want to thank you for leaving the door open for me when
you left.
Now my heart's racing with excitement as I take a deep breath.
Moving on is the next step in my journey.
And being without you will no longer deter me.

My Happy Place

PREFACE

I detailed a lot of emotion throughout this collection, but I think it's important to remember that while some of it was deeply sad and hard for me to live, I have come out better than I was before.

I've met a lot of people on my journey who helped me become the person I am today, and I'm grateful for them. Even the one who broke my heart taught me a lesson and allowed me to realize what I wanted for myself.

I am excited for you to read the last section because it provides a truly happy ending. When you are in the final phases of healing, that's when you can finally open yourself up to someone else, and if it's the right person, it's truly magical.

Trust Me

I look into those discerning eyes, and all I see is blue—
Not just the color, but the sadness that's there, too.
I wish you would confide in me and fully let me in.
But I understand your hesitation because you don't want to
be hurt again.
I know you like to be in charge and have all of the control.
But if you let your guard down with me, it won't make you
weak, but it could make you whole.

Better Together

You're strong, but together we're unbreakable.
You're happy, but together we're in ecstasy.
You're full, but together we're overflowing.
You can live the rest of your days on your own, and I know
you'll be just fine, but with me as your copilot, you'll revel in
this ride we call life.

Here To Stay

I always thought there was something wrong with me that
made everyone walk away.
You made me believe differently when I showed you the door,
but you chose to stay.

Lost In You

Why can't I get you out of my head?
Your smile.
Your eyes.
Your voice.
Everything about you causes something inside of me to break
loose.
I need you to hold on to me, or I might get lost in you.

My Home

You may make my heart soar and continually race.
But I've never been more grounded than when I'm in your
embrace.
Where you are is where I want to be.
And where we are together feels like home to me.

Take A Chance

You're scared, and I'm scared too.
We've both been burned before.
Now we go through this world like ice—numb, hard, and
cold.
But maybe, if we let each other in, we could feel something,
warm our insides, and melt our hearts.
It would be a risk, but it could also set our worlds on fire in the
best possible way.
I think you're worth the chance. What do you say?

My Addiction

I never thought I'd be a person who needed someone else's
attention.
I was content with nothing but my own company.
Then, out of nowhere, you made me reevaluate my intentions.
You woke up a hidden fiend inside of me.
One who is greedy and hopelessly addicted to you.
I'd always thought of myself as selfless.
But I crave to occupy your time and everything you do.
When it comes to wanting you, I'm nothing but selfish.

Claim Me

Tell me what you want; I'll tell you if I want it too.
If it involves just me and you, then chances are I probably do.
Tell me what you think and feel.
I need to know you're for real.
I don't want to hear any lies.
Or you feeding me false alibies.
I want to be the only one.
And know that this isn't just for fun.
I'm so tired of playing this back-and-forth game.
Just end it all and tell me that I'm the one you claim.

I Feel You

I know we don't know each other all that well.
But there's something between us, I can tell.
You're like a shot of serotonin, straight to my brain.
I need you in my life just to keep me sane.
It's weird how the only emotion I ever felt was fine.
But something inside of me opened up the moment I called
you mine.

Perfect Day

We can spend all day under the covers.
Turn off our phones and just enjoy each other.
Lips pressed, bodies caressed, breast to breast.
Make every minute count—there's no time for rest.
We can hide in our blanketed fort away from prying eyes.
Exploring one another from sunrise to sunrise.

Goddess

Keep the lights on. I want to see every inch of you.
From the dimples when you smile all the way to your ankle
tattoo.
Stop worrying about stretch marks or cellulite on your thighs.
You need to know that you're an absolute goddess in my eyes.
I want to worship at your temple, so please let me inside.
Get all those fears out of your head and just enjoy this ride.

Perfect Fit

You're like gasoline to my fire, causing that passion-fueled
desire.
I want you to wake up and think of me, and when you dream,
it's my face you see.
I like that you're obsessive because I am too.
And I can't deny I'm totally infatuated with you.
You encourage me to embrace my excitable nature.
Yet you're a calming agent for my irrational behavior.
You're the yin to my yang on everything that matters.
So please don't leave me because it would be my heart that
shatters.

Right For Me

Watching you sitting there wrapped in a blanket, not a worry
on your mind.
I envy the ease with which you shut off from the world and let
yourself unwind.
Your calming presence actually soothes my restless soul.
I want to bottle your energy and take it everywhere I go.
I may never be like you, but I get to be with you, which is even
better.
You are the water to my fire, and we balance each other.

Love Song

Give me your hand and place it on my heart.
Feel that rhythm? It's my song for you.
It starts slow and even but crescendos the closer you get.
Composed of love—this melody is yours.
No one else could make my insides sing the way you do.
And if you leave, not only will the music die, but so will I.

Safe Place

I can no longer think straight because my brain is spinning like
a cyclone.
You are the keeper my of thoughts—the queen sitting on my
mind's throne.
You offered me love and understanding like nothing I've ever
known.
Even protected my heart as if it were your own.
Sometimes I can physically feel your touch, even when I'm
alone.
No matter where you are in this world, you are always my
home.

Just A Kiss

I grab your hands in mine, our fingers intertwine.
Pulling you close, you lean down—we're nose-to-nose.
I unlace our fingers and place yours on my hips.
You gasp as I cup your cheeks and capture your luscious lips.
I start off feather-soft, going nice and slow but heating up as
we go.
I slide out my tongue, and as if it were a key, you open up
for me.
Wet, hot passion as our mouths dance together.
It's like they were made for each other.
In this moment, I hope you realize all that you've missed.
And I erased the memory of everyone before me with just a
kiss.

Here For You

You pull me in just to push me away.
I think you're scared if I actually stay.
I know you've been hurt, making happiness hard for you to
trust.
But I promise to make those old wounds feel like nothing
more than paper cuts.
I want to be the only medicine you ever need to take.
Be the arms that hold you if your world starts to break.
All the people before me didn't know how to treat you right.
So I'm asking you to give in and not put up a fight.
I want to love you better than you've ever been loved before.
And every day I'm with you, I love you a little more.

Happily Ever After

I know we each have a past that has been shrouded in pain.
But together, these two wounded hearts have learned to love
again.
Our journeys were different, but we ended up where we were
supposed to.
Finding each other was what we were always meant to do.
Now that I have you, I want to spoil you in all the ways that
matter.
Fill your life with nothing but love and give us our happily
ever after.

Consume By You

I dream, and it's almost as if I'm there.
Touching you, cherishing every second of breathing the
same air.
My mind races to all the things we could do.
It's not just physical—I'm so consumed by you.
Let's meet in our minds, one more time, so I can have you
near.
And there, we can make memories that will never disappear.

Together

You're the lyrics in my head, making it hard to sleep.
The chorus that I keep playing on repeat.
Your words are searching for that perfect beat.
I'm the music hoping you find me.
We are beautiful as we stand alone.
But together, we'd be the greatest love song ever known.

Just Us Two

Your eyes tell a thousand stories.
I see all the pain you suffered at the hands of the people
before me.
It seems like that was another lifetime ago.
But I understand you had to go through that to grow.
Life can't always be rainbows and butterflies.
There is some hurt you just can't disguise.
Now that I'm here, we'll start over brand-new.
And this time, we'll make memories with just us two.

Our Secret Place

I feel sleep calling, or is it you in my dreams?
Pulling me under so you can be with me.
I have waited all day for this time together.
And I would wait for many more if you said it could last
forever.
You take me to this other world, a place where reality is
blurred.
It's our secret place that no one else can see.
And when we're there, it's just you and me.
No outsiders allowed, is what you always say.
As we make love until the break of day.

Drunk On You

My body is fully aware of your every move when you're
around.
You make my stomach drop, and I feel like I'm walking on
unsteady ground.
How is it you can make me feel this way?
It's like I fall in love with you all over again each and every day.
I wake up with a foggy head and a racing heart.
Because I'm drunk on you before the day even starts.
You often ask me where you found me.
And I say, "The universe saw what we couldn't see.
Two souls that belonged together for all of eternity."

Silent Assault

My head's a mess, and it's all your fault.
You broke down my walls with your silent assault.
Taking up residency right inside my mind.
When I search my thoughts, you're all I find.
I'm not going to lie. I like what I see.
All I have to do is close my eyes, and you're here with me.
So bring on this all-consuming distraction.
I knew loving you would cause a chain reaction.

Floating

Love changes not only who you are but how you see.
When you're in love, everything around you seems so happy.
You feel lighter, like you're walking on air.
It lifts you up just knowing someone else is there.
It's like you're wrapped in a warm blanket but also a protective
shield.
Love is comforting and impenetrable—it's like a force field.
Everything is different when you're in love—the feeling
consumes you.
Making you realize if you ever lose it, the emptiness will
destroy you.

Riding High

I can't get you off my brain.
It's like loving you has made me insane.
I can't eat, I can't sleep, all I can do is think of you.
You drive me mad and you don't even try to.
I'm obsessive to say the least.
But once I let you in, all of these thoughts were unleashed.
You're running through my bloodstream, keeping me alive.
Giving in to you and this feeling is the only way I can survive.

Acceptance

I have a bad temper—you say I'm fiery.
I'm obsessive—you say I'm passionate.
I'm an emotional roller coaster—you say I have levels.
All of the things I see as flaws, you view them in a better light.
You make every wrong turn from my past seem right.
And I know that must be true.
Because every road I've taken eventually led me to you.

Simple Pleasures

I brush the hair from your eyes as we lie in bed and watch the
sunrise.
Moving closer, we snuggle together under the covers.
Finding peace in our bedroom bunker that no one else can
discover.
Wrapped in each other's arms is where we always want to be.
Nothing can interrupt us because we've dedicated this time to
you and me.

Fallen

You tell me not to let my mind run away with this.
But I can't help that my thoughts are a toxic mess.
If I lost you, I don't know what I'd do.
You say, "Good thing you won't ever have to.
I'm not going anywhere, so please put this to rest."
You pull me close as I cry into your chest.
I never imagined I would ever let down my guard.
But here we are, and I've fallen so fucking hard.

Destiny

We never have to say goodbye because I know we'll always find
each other in another life.
When we met, my soul already knew that it would forever be
connected to you.
You made me believe in things like true love and destiny.
And that maybe the universe created you just for me.
It's like a fairy tale, and you're always my happily ever after.
But I know our story will never end, and this point is just the
first chapter.

Instant Attraction

I still remember the first day we met.
The way I looked at you, I'll never forget.
I was so thirsty that I drank you in.
You stared into my darkened eyes full of lust and sin.
I wanted to be your greatest temptation.
Because being with you would be my only salvation.

Grateful

I always felt something was missing that I just couldn't see.
I walked around this world for years, wishing it would
find me.
Then I met you, and our hearts collided like a massive
explosion.
Our meeting was something the universe had already put into
motion.
It may not be how we would've planned.
But fate has its own ideas that we will never understand.
So instead of cursing the heavens for taking so long to make
you mine.
I'm nothing but grateful that I get to love you in this lifetime.

Devotion

When I think of you, my whole body starts to ache.
I love you so hard, I think I might break.
You are someone who is everything to me and more.
I never understood what love was until you walked through
the door.
I'll give you that all-encompassing, unending devotion.
Thoughts of you take over my mind and my emotions.
Your love is that can't eat, can't sleep, can't breathe without
you kind.
And that was something I never thought I would find.

Virtuous Sin

You have that bad-look-good thing down to an art.
I don't know why I'm surprised even the devil was an angel to
start.
You're the temptation that is constantly pulling me in.
Being with you is like a virtuous sin.
It can't be wrong when everything about it feels so right.
You're my captor and savior, so I don't put up a fight.
Maybe I'm naïve, and I'm under your control.
But being with you is the only thing that makes this broken
heart feel whole.

Rain Dance

Wrapped in my arms, we watch as the sun sets low in the sky.
Out of nowhere, the heavens open, and the angels begin
to cry.
I take your hand and pull you out into the rain.
You seem surprised, but you never once complain.
Holding you close, I say, "Dance with me?"
The water washes over us, and we can barely see.
Swaying to the rhythm of nature, I know I'll never again have
an experience like this.
Making the moment perfect, I pour all of my love into you
when I capture your lips.

Just You

Staring at you in that oversized hoodie,
I knew I'd never seen anyone so sexy.
Sliding my hands up your back and pulling you close.
This fresh-out-of-bed look is how I love you the most.
With your hair all a mess and your face makeup-free.
There is no way I couldn't fall, but I hope that you'll jump
with me.

Living Dream

You look so good lying there in nothing but your sexy
underwear.
Waking up next to you in my bed is like a dream coming to life
straight from my head.
I watch your bare breasts rise as you arch your back.
I think to myself, my God, I could get used to that.
I don't want to close my eyes because I'm afraid you'll
disappear.
But then you snuggle into me, erasing all of my fears.

Alternate Reality

My mind's an illusionist, making me believe you're still here
with me.
Closing my eyes tight, I immerse myself in this alternate
reality.
It's a perfect place and has become my favorite obsession.
Wanting you this much is my secret confession.
My every thought is consumed by you.
I don't know how to shake it, and I'm not sure I want to.
I've become an insomniac because I keep playing you on
repeat.
But if I dream while I'm awake, I might as well try to sleep.

Safe

You say you love how deep I am.
But you stay in the shallow water away from the dam.
Are you scared that it will break and all my emotions will
drown you?
Or are you afraid of yourself and what you might actually do?
Give me your hand and let me guide you into the deepest part
of the sea.
I promise to hold on tight, and you'll realize that you're always
safe with me.

Contentment

"Goodnight." You start to roll over, but I don't want you
to go.
I know I'll see you in the morning, but that time will pass too
slow.
"Please stay here with me for just a minute longer?"
I wrap my arms around you, and maybe next time you try to
leave, my resolve will be stronger.

Shining Light

I see you there, looking so gorgeous, and I can't help but stare.
It's hard to believe that you have this effect on me, but there's
no denying you do.
My breath still hitches every... single... time that I'm with you.
Your soul shines brighter than anything I've ever seen.
And I realize I'm the luckiest person in the world because
you're in love with me.

Missing Piece

I felt lost and broken before I found you.
I went through life not really knowing what to do.
I was going through the motions, just trying to survive.
Getting up each day and pretending to be alive.
Before you, I felt incomplete, like I wasn't whole.
I never knew it was because you had a piece of my soul.

Clarity

I see things inside of you that no one else can see.
I see that I was made for you, and you were made for me.
I need to hold you in my arms each and every night.
I need you forever because you're the only person who feels
right.
I want to know your every craving and desire.
I want to be the flame that sets your world on fire.
I hope you see, need, and want the same things I do.
Because I couldn't imagine my life without you.

Protect Me

You're like the life force running through my veins.
The glue that holds together my broken remains.
You saw me when I was invisible to the rest of the world.
You listened to me when I felt like I couldn't be heard.
I'm not sure where you came from or how you found me.
But you're like an angel, and your wings surround me.
Protecting me from all the harm that others created.
I had worried I wasted my life with the wrong people,
But the truth is, I'm glad that I waited.

This Is Love

Take me to your happy place.
Open up and let me inside—not just your mind and body, but
your heart.
Let me show you what love looks like when neither of us has
to hide,
And we are both honest from the start.
I know we have issues because we've been hurt before.
But those days are over now, and we can finally close that
door.
Let me show you that people can keep their promises and be
true.
I know we all have our missing piece out there.
And I want mine to be you.

Forever Mine

I'd never been lucky in love until I saw you standing there.
Meeting you was like the universe answering a prayer.
There are people who long to experience the way you make me
feel.
My heart breaks for them because a love like this is surreal.
But, together, we're unstoppable as our souls have
become one.
We have an unbreakable bond that can never be undone.
They say a love like this only comes once in a lifetime.
But I know we'll meet again because you're forever mine.

Afterword

If you made it this far, I hope you were satisfied with the outcome. Life will always take us on unexpected rides, but if you have the right people by your side, you'll feel safer when those bumps in the road happen—and they will continue to happen.

It took me a long time to see that people don't change, no matter how much love you give them. So pouring yourself into the wrong people will leave you empty and sad. I think we've all been there before, whether it's friendship or more. But the thing I learned the most is that even though there are those people out there who will break you, there are also people out there who will save you. When you get hurt, you can't become bitter and never want to put yourself out there again, or you'll never know what it's like to feel whole.

If you are ever experiencing a time in your life where you feel lost, maybe read some of my words from "Marks of Sadness" and realize you're not alone. Or if you're going through a stage of learning to trust again, check out "Healing Grace" and you'll find that there are people who will pick you up when you're down. And anytime you just want to feel good or that excitement of what new love is like, then take a look back at "My Happy Place."

When I set out to write this, I had a goal in mind. I wanted whoever picked it up to feel like no matter what stage they were at in life, they could relate to something in here. And maybe after reading this, you found hope that things will always get better.

Acknowledgments

I want to thank everyone who took this journey with me, and I hope you all find peace and happiness.

About the Author

Abigail Taylor is a contemporary LGBTQ+ romance author and self-confessed music junkie. She's a workout enthusiast who has completed several Tough Mudders where she swam in ice baths and was even electrocuted.

She loves doing things outside of her comfort zone and pushing boundaries, but when it comes to romance, she loves a happy ending!

Abigail enjoys traveling the world, meeting new people, and trying new experiences such as jumping from a plane at 9,000 feet, but for now, she's busy giving life to her characters.

Thank you for all of your support!

You can keep in contact with me through:

- Email (abbytaylorauthor@gmail.com)
- Instagram (@abbytaylorauthor)
- Twitter (twitter.com/a_taylorauthor)
- Facebook (facebook.com/abigailtaylorauthor)
- Amazon (amazon.com/author/abigailtaylor)
- Website (abbytaylorauthor.wixsite.com/website)

Also by Abigail Taylor

LOOKING FOR LOVE SERIES

Forever Love (Book 1)

First Love (Book 2)

Fighting Love (Book 3)

Finding Love (Book 4)

STANDALONE

She's Home

FREE STORY

A New Direction

Printed in Great Britain
by Amazon

79107182R00098